Will USA Prostitute Away Our Sovereignty, we already owe 16 trillion and counting, there is no telling what we may have to give up at some point? When you are dependent like that you may have to beg, borrow, steal, and do no telling what else just to survive, the liberals with their welfare state did this to this great nation, what a shame.

I am a completely self-made writer and you have to take my writing as is, no hired editor here just my crude, raw, and uncut message, sorry.

Government in the role of social and family provider doesn't work and is an impossible task. Sure, almost any system may last 80-100 years. Like I have said before, in my opinion there is no system known to man more dangerous to long term survive than the welfare state, not communism, socialism, or any other system.

It lulls all but a few into a false sense of security to depend on an all powerful government until it is too late. Nature's supreme law of "Natural selection" is based on a survival need to determine what exist or start ceasing to exist. So, if there is no survival need for the strong nuclear and extended family to exist it becomes weaker and weaker until it is out of existence.

The welfare state takes away the survival

need for the nuclear and extended family thereby completely destroying a nations and culture leaving no way to survive if the welfare state collapses, and it will.

Government and the welfare state survive only from the profit made by businesses and a business can't survive unless it makes a profit. It stands to reason that the bigger government gets the bigger bite it must take out of a businesses profit and at some point it will kill the business.

Americans business can't support our welfare state beast and at some point we can't borrow another penny, then guess what, your guess is as good as mine. The only hope as I see it is to eliminate the minimum wage and start a process of letting the people learn how to start surviving again on their own. God save this great land of the free and home of the brave. Amen.
SIRMANS LOG: 4 APRIL 2012, 1307 HOURS

READ MY SHORT RAW NO CHASER LECTURE ON SIRMANS ECONOMICS!
It never ceases to amaze me on just how economically ignorant most people are. This whole modern generation is looking to big government to always be there to take care of them. But, the true fact is the government is only a necessary parasite that every organized society must have to defend and

2

protect its citizens.

An Economy consists of only to parties, a seller and a buyer or a merchant and a consumer. Nature's supreme law of "Natural selection" balances these two forces against each other where prices can never get out of hand.

If government just take a small amount off the top a balance can still be maintained, but, when government takes too much of the cream of profit the incentive to produce heads downward. The government doesn't generate any profit and every penny it takes in taxes to survive originates from some form of private business transaction.

It is either directly or indirectly. Non business people that pay taxes to the government all receive their pay from some form of private business transaction profit. So, what have we now, a general public that see government as some kind of imaginary omnipotent sow with countless tits that we can suck on forever.

That is sheer madness and to top that we have this liberal anti-business climate that bites the hand that feeds it. My God! It is a case of the parasite attacking the host that keeps it alive, how dumb and stupid can it get? This is what the shallow minded liberals and their welfare state has done to this great predominate Christian nation.

There has never been a mass social and family provider government in the history of mankind before the "New deal" came along. The profits from private enterprise are what supports government and can keep government supplied as long as government limits its spending to national defense and the infrastructure.

But, the profit from private business can never be enough to support a social and provider government very long. The welfare state days are over, it is no mystery to me, there is simply not enough business profit to pay the cost, and you can't get blood out of a turnip, period. And anybody that think that we as a nation can continue with our welfare state is living in fantasy land, period.

It is simply impossible to pay the cost, we are broke people, and still we have politicians in washing acting like we are a rich nation. We are over 16 trillion in debt and still trying to spend like drunken sailors.

The egg heads with scrambled brains and the elite will never change course they are in a state of denial and will go down with the ship first. And I'm supposed to be the fool and nut case and maybe I am, but at least I have enough common sense to know we are headed toward total doom.

I write what I think and believe, so I hope my short lecture will enlighten at least one soul somewhere out there and everyone won't think I am totally insane.

When I talk about economics I'm talking about a free market place. There has never been a communist or socialist form of government that could feed all of it people. In those types of governments the top leadership lives high on the hog while the general population barley keeps from starving.
SIRMANS LOG: 30 MARCH 2012, 0017 HOURS

QUICK WORD OF KNOWLEDGE INJECTION: Economically speaking caring for the poor or anybody must be kept separated for a free market place to work, that is the problem now, you can't have unlimited individual government spending standing between the merchants and the consumers and expect a healthy sound free market place economy. What you will have is uncontrolled consumer inflation like what is taking place now, that and the "Minimum wage" is the fuel that is spinning consumer inflation out of control.

There is no way in the hell to stop this economy from expanding beyond control and collapse from it own weight with the course it is on. You don't have to take my advice; the

wait won't be very much longer.
Government must sell off damn near
everything and give up its social and family
provider role, period. Will it happen, no?

If the USA government doesn't eliminate the
"Minimum wage and give up its social and
family provider role will the USA economy
survive, no. So, what is going to happen to
this great land of the free and home of the
brave, you really don't want to know the
answer to that as I see it.

Well, if you insist and won't take no for an
answer I guess I have no choice but to tell
you what I think is going to happen. I believe
to buy time and avoid biting the dust our
Welfare State and the Federal Reserve as co-
conspirators will finish selling off what is left
of our freedom and sovereignty to some
foreign highest bidder like a cheap street
walker. And we will end up as debt slaves.

So, how you like me now?
SIRMANS LOG: Last update 27 MARCH 2012,
1613 HOURS

DOES IT REALLY MATTER WHO WINS IN
NOVEMBER???
NEW INJECTION 1
I know people are thinking what about the
government paying off this or that and who is

going to lose this or that. This nation is way past that now we are now in a priority struggle on whether this nation and freedom will survive or be lost forever.

To continue on the doomsday course we are on now soon nothing is going to get paid anyway because we may not even have a country. The shallow minded liberals starting with the "New deal" got this nation in the fix we are in, and even to this day won't accept responsibility for anything but instead can blame the sweetness out ginger bread.

Hell, the liberal ain't over twenty percent of the population, but they are super aggressive, if you get between a liberal and a cause you are going to get trampled if you ain't got your s... together. These people will stop at nothing, morally or otherwise to stay in power.

Someway somehow conservatives must snatch the reins from these people otherwise we are all going over the cliff or down the tube. God save our freedom.
20 MARCH 2012, 2226 HOURS

if you want my opinion, which no one has asked, but, guess what, I'm going to give it anyway. We have a milestone election coming up in November and I believe it will determine whether we as a nation lose our freedom quickly or go the drip by drip route.

The drip by drip course is the best course only because it buys more time for a miracle to possibly save our freedom. OK, OK, what if we do get a new team? What will it do about the welfare state entitlement load?

Will it have the guts to actually lighten the welfare state massive financial load? Sure, I have heard promises about cutting government spending but it ain't gonna happen, the welfare state is simply just too powerful. Besides, in my view making massive cuts in government spending would do more harm than good because all it would do is increase the dole roll?

The problem is government as a social and family provider simply doesn't work and it is impossible to keep it from collapsing soon. The only thing that is going to save the USA and western civilization is to somehow get the government out of its social and family provider role, period.

Otherwise, I don't care what those in powers tell you the USA economy can't be saved, I know almost no one will believe me and why they should, an unknown writer like me can't possibly know jack. An economy is like life itself there must be constant small purges and rebirths taking place for it to stay healthy.

The free market place ideology allows that to take place better than any other economic system known to man. Governments tend not to adhere to supply and demand and will use its power to stop small purges and will reward its friends, thereby choking off healthy small purges and rebirth.

This process won't kill an economy on the spot but will cause it to wither and die on the vine, which is what is happening to the USA and welfare states all over the world. Growth itself is a process of birth and death; otherwise there would be no lasting life.

The welfare state is what is going to destroy the USA and western civilization unless they get out of their social and provider roles. The nuclear and extended family unit is what civilization is based on. It is the foundation of all civilization.

Before the "New deal" the head of household was not only a provider he instilled in the young self-restraint, responsibility, and accountability. The "New deal" birthed the welfare state we have today.

The welfare state on a massive scale has taken the family provider role away from where it had been for over 5,000 years, with each nuclear family unit head of household.

9

That in itself wasn't so bad but what was so destructive even to this day is government as family provider is not making sure the young is instilled with self-restraint, responsibility, and accountability. Only the provider has the power and authority to make sure the young are prepared to be productive future adults.

Today with the poor it is not uncommon to see grand and great grand mothers having to raise young kids. I just highlighted a sample of the destruction the welfare state has done just on our culture. Moving on to some of the destruction the welfare state has done to our economy.

The founding fathers knew what an all powerful big government would do they had seen it back in old Europe. They knew that the only way to control government was to keep it small. The constitution is all about limiting the power of government over the people.

The constitution gave the greatest power to the people and to the states. The state governors use to have awesome powers. Each state governor appointed two senators to represent his and the state's interest.

Then because of petty politics, with the 17th amendment the states gave up their real power by not having two appointed senators to represent only state business and interest, now special interest may have more influence with the senators than the state governor. And the people gave up their real power by allowing the government to take over the family provider role for itself.

Now the all powerful welfare state with little to no real opposition is busy consolidating its massive power to finish selling off the little sovereign power the USA has left. Within five years the USA will be an economic slave in my opinion, now chew on that.

Whoever is the provider has the power to be the boss, yes sir. In economic terms the only thing that truly matters is profit. You can be spinning your wheels and kicking up all kinds of dust but if you are not making any profit you ain't going anywhere.

As a country when we are borrowing forty cents of every dollar we spend we are definitely profit challenged. Every cent the government takes comes from some type of private business transaction. When government is small it only needs to take a small amount out of a businesses profit margin. But, the bigger government grows the more it must take from the profit a business makes.

This welfare state we have won't stop until its bite is so big no business can make a profit, there is no stopping the greed of a welfare state. It don't make any sense, that doesn't matter, most of the stuff taking place now don't make any sense in my view.

No matter who wins the election if they are not willing to get the government out of its super provider role it will not save this economy. Here is what should be done, first eliminate the "Minimum wage."

Next set up government run commissaries, government housing, and government run clinics with the use of token or script for those that qualify.

Lastly, government must stop giving out free money or food stamps to anyone that is what driver consumer inflation and keeps prices sky high for everyone.
SIRMANS LOG: 18 MARCH 2012, 0014 HOURS

STOP MASS MURDER OF THE INNOCENT IN THE WOMB
What few people understand about freedom and a free market place is it works both ways; there must be freedom to succeed or fail, and freedom to pay the most in wages or the least.

That is what freedom means, without force in any direction that is what nature's supreme law of "Natural selection" is all about, without force, let nature's law of "Natural selection" decides. That means an employer should have the right to pay as much or as little as he wants to as long as no force is involved, no one has to accept it.

The greatest and mightiest of giant oak trees started as a small acorn. The ability to start small is what real growth is all about. Before all of the big government welfare states bars and hoops one has to jump through now any poor person with initiative could pull himself up by his own boot straps.

Now starting from almost nothing is becoming almost impossible and is only going to get worse. Sure, I write a lot of extreme stuff, which to a large extent is to stress a point, but, I know the secret to life is all about balance and common sense.

Like in time of old, the people knew without a doubt that certain things doesn't chance with time and one of those things was building character.

We as humans have evolved over millions of years through hardship and struggle. And I just don't believe that a strong survival instinct along with good judgment and character can be instilled in the young without a certain amount of real or imposed hardship and struggle.

Of all the crimes against nature the welfare state has done I think the biggest of all is its corruption of the poor. Never in the history of mankind has the poor been moral corrupted on such a mass scale and is out there killing babies in the womb by the millions, may God bless their souls.
SIRMANS LOG: 15 MARCH 2012, 1425 HOURS

LET THE SUPREME COURT RULE ON THE CONSTITUTIONALITY OF THE "MINIMUM WAGE."
Mandates, mandates, individual mandates, and mandates to no end. When it comes to individual mandates to make everyone buy health insurance or go to jail I am against that along with almost everyone.

Well, what about one of the first individual government mandates, I'm talking about the "Minimum wage, that was one of the welfare states first mandates. Without the minimum wage the welfare state could never have taken over and grown into this all powerful monster we have today that is going to spend this nation into oblivion.

If I am willing to work for someone just for room and board why shouldn't I have that right? If I am willing to pay all of someone's expense and pay them a dollar a day why shouldn't they have a right to say yes/no.

In today's climate I know it would be a miracle to pass a Supreme Court decision, still, I think it should be put to a Supreme Court test. As you can see, I am totally against a "Minimum wage" I think getting rid of the minimum wage especially at this late stage is the only thing that will save the USA and western civilization, period.
SIRMANS LOG: 14 MARCH 2012, 2041 HOURS

WHAT IS MORAL DECAY? DUH!
One of the reasons I am so misunderstood is because I have a super strong survival instinct, whereas today due to the welfare state most Americans has a dependency weak survival instinct.

You first have to know and be able to recognize a moral threat before you can truly take someone like me serious; I am mostly dismissed and seen as some kind of nut case talking a lot of hate filled nonsense. Which, couldn't be farther from the truth?

I understand this because not all has paid the price in struggle and suffering that I have to instill a super survival instinct. But, history is my guide and without a doubt will prove me right.

Anything that doesn't protect the unborn and

future generations is a moral threat in my eyes, by instinct alone I just know, no one has to tell me. A moral threat doesn't physical kill you on the spot but over time it is just as dangerous, your species will cease to exist.

No sovereign country can continue to depend forty percent on another and stay free and independent for very long. Almost everyone is totally focused on the lack of jobs and the economy while what is coming in low under the radar is just as destructive.

I am talking about moral decay and culture rot. Anyone with any knowledge of history should know that moral decay and culture rot is the last stage before a nation will be taken over or conquered.

Throughout history the only real security for women, children, the elderly, and everyone else has been with a strong nuclear and extended family system. But, here we are as a nation putting all of our faith in a welfare state that is on life support, God help us.

Almost the whole nation is in mass denial from being brainwashed for decades by a liberal bias news media in my view. I am totally in favor of women rights as well as rights for all Americans, but there is not going to be rights for any of us if we don't first save our nuclear and extended family system and our culture.

This country's government is borrowing forty cents out of every dollar it spends, and what is even worse is nothing is being done about it, and even super worse is we have a liberal bias media that is on the sideline cheering the process on, God save us.

No country with a culture like we had before the "New deal" would tolerate this behavior for one second, which is proof of what this welfare state beast has done to our once great culture.

The moral decay and culture rot due to our welfare state has just grown too powerful; only the elimination of the "Minimum wage" will set in motion a process that will save the United States of America.
SIRMANS LOG: 11 MARCH 2012, 1425 HOURS

CURRENT EVENT INJECTION:
THERE IS BLOOD IN THE WATER AND THE LIBERAL SHARKS ARE CIRCLING!
The great conservative radio talk show host has admitted that he slipped up and has apologized for the infractions. He is not the first one to get caught up in emotion and stray over the line and will not be the last.

However, the progressive liberals smell blood

in the water and in their view sees this as their opportunity to take down the biggest conservative voice of all. Sure, they already got the heat turned up enough to drive a few from the kitchen, but, in my view they are kicking around a powder keg, here.

This could rejuvenate and give life to a dying moral decaying giant that is all but dead in America. Sure, in my view the radio talk show host was wrong for his slut and prostitute name calling, but, he was right on his assault on the outrageous moral decay that is rotting to the core our once great culture.

The shallow minded liberals don't know what the hell I'm talking about concerning moral decay, they couldn't recognize a moral threat if it slapped them upside the head. I could go on and on but enough said, I say let bygones be bygones. I rest my case.
SIRMANS LOG: 6 MARCH 2012, 0024 HOURS

PS: JUST A PASSING THOUGHT, 8 marches 2012, 2345 HOURS:
I think one of the major TV networks has morphed into just a plain negative anti-survival moral decay propaganda machine. I believe this TV network has contempt and a secret hate for the strong traditional nuclear family. And especially one with a no nonsense strong male disciplinarian as head of

household.

GOVERNMENT SPENDING AIN'T THE
PROBLEM; HOW IT DOES THE SPENDING IS
THE PROBLEM.
Just like the big powerful enemy armored
divisions of WWII ran on ball bearings the
welfare state runs on the "Minimum wage.
So, the only way the people is ever going to
regain control and save the last bastion of
true freedom of the individual left in the
world today is by completely eliminating the
minimum wage, period.

The all powerful welfare state beast will never
in its view yield one inch of its God given
power back to the people; it will see this
country in ashes first. It all starts with the
minimum wage; I'm talking about the growth
and taking over of the country by the welfare
state. The minimum wage is the life blood
and backbone of the welfare state.

Without the minimum there would be no out
of control welfare state beast like we have
today. Without the minimum wage anyone
could hire the poor, the young, the
handicapped, the prisoners, and many, many
others without facing mountains of red tape.
As it is now everyone must pay a minimum
wage, and meet every other kind of
government restriction one can imagine.

Without the minimum wage you wouldn't have the elderly, single women, single men, and probably a fifth of the USA population living alone. Once government got a taste of the God like power of being a super social and family provider and playing daddy without carrying out family discipline the die was cast for the destruction of our culture.

Nowhere in over five thousand years of written history has government ever been a mass social and family provider until the "New deal" came along. The government now takes from self-sacrificing hardworking producers and in many cases gives that hard earned money to lack of initiative deadbeat non-producers. My God! People are not stupid! How long will it be before the country is reduced to the lowest denominator?

Truly we are living on borrowed time. The minimum wage must go if western civilization is to survive; there are no ifs, and's, and but's about it. It is not possible for prices to rise above what the poor can afford to pay unless government is subsidizing price raising on an individual basis in some way.

Government giving anyone free money or food stamps is subsiding price raising on the general public no matter how you spin it, the result is still the same, consumer inflation. As a last resort, if the government must aid the poor it can be done without causing out of control inflation like we have today.

If government must aid the poor and disadvantage it should be done by establishing government run Commissaries, housing, and clinics and issue tokens or script to those that qualify. That will prevent out of control consumer inflation like we have today.

That will allow the rest of the working poor and others to pay for their own food and doctor bills. Then almost all of the money government takes in taxes can go to repairing bridges, the highways, city pipe and sewage systems and above all adequate national defense.

The people are suppose to be taking care of the government not the government taking care of the people, and especially not in masses like this welfare state is doing. I say to hell with the eggheads and the elites with their doomsday go down with the ship insanity, I say lets stop this suicide train to hell by first eliminating the minimum wage.

That will quickly bleed the pressure off the stuck inflationary throttle. Then with the minimum wage no reverse restriction bar lifted a true free market place economy will kick in and back this run-a-way mother away from the cliff. Whew! Just in time! Thank God!

There is never a case in history where a real true free market place economy failed. Sure, it rebirths and renews itself but that is normal to get rid of waste and inefficiency. That is what is wrong with our welfare state, the moral decay and liberal media bias has a deadly choke hold on this nation that only a free market place with normal rebirths can break. Otherwise, a total economic collapse is imminent.

I don't need or want any credit for anything, I'm just hell bent on doing what I can to help save my homeland, the only home I know. Praise be to God.
SIRMANS LOG: 25 FEBRUARY 2012, 2140 HOURS

THE BIG LIE STIMULUS FALSE ASSUMPTION!
NEW INJECTION 2:
The reason I know without a doubt that I am right on most of the things I write about is because the economy is just like life itself; it must have a death and rebirth cycle. It is like having a normal healthy memory, in order to have that we must be able to prioritize and forget ninety nine percent of the junk and meaningless stuff we experience.

We know that oxidation work to get rid of things physically. I'm not for sure what get rid of things mentally but I do know by nature's design everything must fail or die or be renewed in some way or cease to exist.

Moral decay, inefficiency, and waste must be gotten rid of or they will become too powerful and bring down civilization itself, which could mean back to the Stone Age. The only way to save the USA is by eliminating the "Minimum wage" and reverting back to a true free market place economy with unrestricted competition.

The moral decay, the partisan liberal news media, and other anti-survival forces have become just too powerful for the USA to survive as a free people, period. Nothing except a true free market place can do the weeding without throwing out the baby with the bath water.
19 FEBRUARY 2012, 1625 HOURS
NEW INJECTION 1:

There is probably a divine reason why I keep up the drum beat of a complete elimination of the "Minimum wage." You see, man using reasoning and intelligence will never get the USA out of the economically mess the progressive liberals has gotten this nation into.

Only God and natures supreme law of "Natural selection" can save the USA and the world from total destruction back to the

Stone Age. That is the reason I keep screaming, get rid of the "Minimum wage" at all cost, because I know man with his facts and figures alone will never save our civilization, it is too far gone.

There are simply just too many variables many which are subjective like whose back is being scratched, who is hiding under the desk, and on and on. That is why power hates a free market place because it prevents the handing out of goodies to cronies.

The invisible hand which is nature's supreme law of "Natural selection" in action is what ultimately rules the economy and all existence anyway. "You can't get blood out of a turnip," the laws of nature are just that simple and to think and do otherwise is a state of denial.

All the elimination of the "Minimum wage" does is set in motion what is going to ultimately happen by the force of nature anyway. But, if Mother Nature is force to carry out its law it could mean back to the Stone Age.

18 FEBRUARY 2012, 0945 HOURS
I got so sick and tired of hearing this big lie about how worse off the economy would be if not for the stimulus that I just couldn't take it anymore, I just had to vent.

People getting on TV talking about how bad the economy would be today if not for the trillions of dollars spent on the stimulus package. Nonsense, the truth is most of that spending went to phony liberal crony capitalism anyway in my view.

What they keep saying is an unprovable assumption but with the general public being so ignorant on how a free market place actually works it allows the liberals to keep running their phony shell game. All of that money was actually wasted and did far more damage to the economy.

Proof of why it actually did more damage than good is what it did to government. The sound free market place formula is very simple, more and bigger government is bad because that means government must take even more of the dwindling profit businesses are struggling to survive on.

It not only took the nation trillions deeper into debt it vastly increased the growth in government which makes the nation and the economy far worse off than before the stimulus.

The fact is more and bigger government is bad, and smaller and lesser government is good if this nation is to survive, but, of course, trying to get a shallow minded liberal to understand something so simple is a horse of a different color.

So, the real proof is instead of the stimulus package saving the USA economy it stepped up the pace of the slow death watch we are on. The day of reckoning looms on the horizon. Like a broken record I must throw this in, the elimination of the minimum wage will force this nation to save itself, there is no other option.

My great wisdom and destiny demands I keep sounding my same stress call "The elimination of the minimum wage is a must, period," with love always.
SIRMANS LOG: 17 FEBRUARY 2012, 1854 HOURS

LESSER OF TWO EVILS AND LIKING IT!
I am not a scheming or devious type person and don't think in those terms, but, there are some who do and is very good at it. In politics there is a very old tactic and I think Richard M. Nixon honed it almost to a science with submitting Supreme Court justices.

First you trot out someone or something extreme that you know probably won't be accepted, then when the noise die down you ease in your real intent and it will be gladly accepted. Just a little food for thought, that is all, good day.

SIRMANS LOG: 12 FEBRUARY 2012, 1700 HOURS.

CURRENT EVENT INJECTION 19 JANUARY 2012: KEYSTONE OIL PIPELINE DECISION! I definitely don't need this, I would be far better off keeping my personal view to my self on this matter, but, I guess I'm a motor mouth at times and can't help it.

Anyone that has ever read any of my writing knows that I'm for small government and totally against a welfare state type government. That means that I disagree almost one hundred percent of the time with the current administrations policies. But, on this Keystone Pipeline issue I must admit that I totally agree with their decision on this.

Experts have been wrong before and will be wrong again, that is a given. Why take a chance and risk destroying the water supply of three states when it can be avoided. Sure, the cost is going to be much higher and take longer, but later saying that shouldn't have happen, or saying we are sorry won't bring back clean water.

I have personally experienced Murphy's Law in action many times. Murphy's Law says if anything bad can possibly happen it will. I think the risk is just far too great no matter what the experts say when you are talking about the water supply of three states.

To me it is a no brainier, just go around the aquifer. Sure, we are desperate in need of jobs but first we must have clean water to live.

CURRENT EVENT INJECTION 19 JANUARY 2012:
WHAT A DREAM TEAM?
Newt + JC

CURRENT EVENT INJECTION 16 JANUARY 2012!
THE CRUISE LINE INCIDENT:
MY BIGGEST SURPRISE AND MAYBE A BIGGER QUESTION IS:
Why would a modern ship like that go down so fast? I thought in modern ship building at least some type of compartmentalized structure would be in place, but, again what do I know, maybe it is too cost prohibitive. No matter how well trained the crew, a ship going down that fast with that many people there are going to be problems.

DISSECTING USA ECONOMY
Like I've said many times, I can dissect an economy as well as anyone. Here is my bold brash opinion on the options if the USA and western civilization is to survive.

The way I see the situation in the USA is first things first and I've yet to hear anyone hit the target. To talk about getting out of debt or saving our freedom while government is still in the role of super social and family provider in my view is dumb and stupid.

That is something that is impossible, we are lucky that this has lasted this long. You see, government doesn't have any money and every penny it takes comes from some type of business profit. The bigger government gets the more profit it must take from businesses until it kills off all business profit. We are not there yet, but we are headed there at warp speed.

Sure, government taxes the people and almost everything else that exist, but where do the people get there money, ultimately like I said all income leads back to some type of business transaction.

A society must have some type of government for internal and external protection of the whole society otherwise government wouldn't be needed. Government is not part of an economy it is just a parasite needed for protection. In simple terms, an economy consists of only two players, a seller and a buyer no matter how modern or complicated it may seem.

Starting with the seller, using some form of energy the seller produces a product or service and a buyer purchases it. An employee himself is actually a seller, he sell his labor for a paycheck. A business itself is only a medium of exchange to generate a profit for the owner, if it doesn't generate a profit it can't exist.

To sum it up, government is only needed to protect society, but, it has the big guns and the power to take over and some do. And believe it or not with the course we are on that is exactly what is going to happen to the great USA, it is only logic.

Unless we start by eliminating the minimum wage and void practically all regulations the economy is guaranteed to totally collapse. After that there will be mass hunger, rioting in the streets and a lot of people being shot, then the people themselves will demand that government take over.

However, with the eliminating of the minimum wage and choking regulations government won't collapse, but it will severely deflate and a lot of rich people will go broke. But, we will save out freedom and survive, it won't be easy but the people will regain control and the nation will survive.

Otherwise, with the course we are on freedom and the nation will be lost forever.

There it is y'all all wrapped and packaged, you don't have to agree with me but that is my brief analysis.

Sure, government shouldn't be in the role of super social and family provider, but, when all else has failed government does has a responsibility to not let the poor freeze or starve. However, government also should never hand out free unearned money or food stamps to the poor or anyone else if the free market place is to survive.

The only way government can help the poor without destroying the nuclear family, the culture, and the economy is to establish government runs commissaries, housing, and clinics with the use of tokens or script for those who qualify.

Government handing out free cash and food stamps guarantees a big enough pool of paying customers where the merchant don't ever have to lower prices, thereby causing higher prices and taxes on everyone. That is what's causing this out of control consumer inflation that is killing us today.

Government can spend all it wants to and it won't cause consumer inflation unless money is handed out on an individual basis, the individual basis is what destroys the natural balance between the buyer and the seller.

I will tell any conservative, okay, you want small government, well; you can't get there from here. First, where you start is fight to eliminate the minimum wage and void countless choking regulations that will get you there, there is no other way, period. SIRMANS LOG: 10 JANUARY 1727, 1005 HOURS

In sheer economic terms government as a social and family provider and having a lasting free market place at the same time simply don't mix, it is like pouring water in acid. It not only destroys a free market place economy it corrupts morals and leaves a nations culture in total ruins.

Look what the welfare state has done to the great USA, we are totally broke with trillions of dollars in debt which makes us slaves to foreign sources. And what is even scarier is we have a shallow hype prone predominate liberal news media that has left the general public totally in the dark on the true state of the nation.

With little to no nuclear and extended family foundation left and any minimum bartering capacity to sustain us under distress, this nation could become authoritarian or a dictatorship almost overnight.

In my opinion with the czars already in place

and with a shallow predominate liberal news media that can't recognize a moral or deep threat if it slapped them upside the head, the only thing now saving the last bastion of true freedom in the world today is the second amendment. And its days are probably numbered.

All of which could be avoided if the minimum wage was eliminated and all big government regulations were voided and then added back as needed. We as a nation are like fools with all of our eggs still in one giant big government welfare state basket, how sad, God help us.

Around the world I imagine many are amused by the fix we are in. But, at the same time they are in almost boot shaking fear, because wise men know the most dangerous thing there is, is when a great nation is injured or losing power.
05 JANUARY 2012, NEW INJECTION:

<u>My God! Maybe my deep wisdom is greater than even I realize.</u> A thing about the economy that seems so simple to me doesn't even register with the so called highly intelligent great economic thinkers of today.

I listen every day on this and that and what this politician is going to do to fix the economy and on and on. While at the same time welfare states all over the world is in the early stages of collapsing down upon their heads.

Still, the powers that be don't even have a clue as to the one and only thing that can save the USA and western civilization. I believe the global economy is past the stage of no return, it can't be saved, but at least western civilization itself can be saved if this one and only thing is done.

The one and only thing that I know without a shadow of doubt that will save western civilization is "Get government out of the role of social and family provider, period." However, after eighty years of ever increasing big government dependency that is an almost impossible task.

Also, another go against the grain widely held false assumption that flies in the face of sound economics is the belief that the "Minimum wage is a good thing." In economic terms the minimum wage is destructive wishful thinking, period. The minimum wage doesn't increase wealth it only distorts wealth and kills the free market place.

The minimum wage makes what cost $5.00 after awhile cost $50.00. The only thing that increases wealth is the increase in production and buying power. Without the elimination of the minimum wage it will be impossible to get the government out of its family provider role to save western civilization.

Power will always go down with the ship, only divine intervention can save us now, God help us. Government in the role of social and family provider given time will always kill an economy. It is done by taking too much profit leaving no incentive for anyone to go into or stay in business.

Given time big government will also snuff out all greed and self-interest which leaves no incentive to produce except by the whip. With the whip one will produce only enough to stay alive which is the history of communism and socialism.

So, there it is in a nut shell folks, you have the facts and a solution. You can dismiss me, the facts, and everything else I say, but you won't prove me wrong.
SIRMANS LOG: 04 JANUARY 2012, 1220 HOURS

CURRENT EVENT INJECTION!
THE PAYROLL TAX CUT EXTENSION:
Some people are coming down hard on the house speaker saying he is a caver and can't stand up to pressure. Well, I for one totally disagree; I think he made the right decision on avoiding a tax raise on the American people.

Sure, the liberals are demagoguing the issue but that is expected and beside the point. You have a general public that is 95 percent ignorant on economic matters; they can't see past their noses and will be film flamed almost every time by the liberals, what is one to do.

With the liberals and their cohorts in the new media pouring on the demagoguery there is no doubt that will get the blame? Educating the public is the only real solution but that is no easy task after eighty years of big government liberal do-for-me entitlement propaganda.

Facing unreasonable odds a wise man will try to live to fight another day hopefully on terms more to his favor. "Fools rush in where wise men fear to tread."
SIRMANS LOG: 24 DECEMBER 2011, 0055 HOURS

WITH NO MINIMUM WAGE THE RICH HAS THE MOST TO LOSE THE POOR IS ALREADY DIRT POOR!
Here is the skinny on this minimum wage thing I keep harping on. Sure, I know almost everybody is thinking that I'm a fool and don't know what the hell I'm talking about, and besides, they feel it will never happen anyway. And they are probably right because

I have no power to make anyone do anything.

Plus, everybody keep thinking that it don't make sense because the poor can't make it as is, they need to raise the minimum wage not get rid of it. Wrong, wrong, wrong, it is just the opposite and I so happen to be one of the very few with the wisdom and perspective to see it.

Without the minimum wage the welfare state beast will get starved out of its cradle to grave super provider role. Without government driving up and keeping prices high by giving money and food stamps to the poor it would be impossible for prices to go above what the poor can afford because there is never enough rich to keep commerce flowing.

Sure, government must help the very poor and not let people starve but it can be done without destroying our culture and economy like what the welfare state has done. The way you help the poor and not destroy the culture, the economy, freedom, and everything else is by establishing government run commissaries, housing, and clinics.

Plus, tokens or script must be issued to those that qualify to keep from contaminating the national free market place currency. The reason for that is there are only two players in an economy they are the <u>seller and buyer,</u> or the <u>merchant and consumer</u>.

Government was created to guard and protect the process plus the whole society. However, government has the big guns and the fighters, so, without an armed populace it is a lot easier for a tyrant to try to seize power and take over.

Through natures supreme law of "Natural selection" the <u>buyer and seller</u> will always keep a natural balance between the two. But, when government put in a minimum wage and all kind of regulations it destroys the balance between the <u>buyer</u> and the <u>seller</u>.

The government creates consumer inflation by giving enough <u>buyers</u> (poor) the money to afford super high prices. The <u>merchant</u> then get away with raising prices because government is paying a large enough pool to allow it, otherwise prices would have to remain lower enough for most poor folks to pay their own doctor and food bills.

Once government got a taste of being a provider it got drunk on the control and power of lording it over people. So, it decide to create the great society, food stamps and everything else from cradle to grave, no problem, just raise taxes a little higher.

While all of this was going on the rich and the

very poor had it made while consumer inflation was eating the middle class alive. To tell the truth folks, I don't know how things will finally play out if the minimum is eliminated. But, I do know that if it is not eliminated we will lose our freedom and maybe even our country.

I don't have to be right and no one may agree with anything I write, still, this is the way I see it.
SIRMANS LOG: 17 DECEMBER 2011, 0014 HOURS

WHY THE POOR CAN'T CREATE SOME OF THEIR OWN JOBS. OK, OK, I hear you America! This is what big government and the welfare state has brought us to. I think it's going to come down to first just eating and surviving. I think it is better to eat and survive than to have untold amounts of gold and riches and starve.

Once there is no threat of starving then the sky can be the limit. I'm going to go out on a limb and say something that is taboo and political incorrect way beyond measure. I'm saying there is a place for "Roles" in life provided they are not set in stone and there is freedom of choice.

Throughout history until the "New deal" and the welfare state the children, the sick, and the elderly were always taken care of in a healthy and stable environment. To me it is a given the welfare state is now collapsing down upon us I see it and know it but the egg heads and elites will never admit it until it is too late.

So, what are we going to do about being prepared when we know a change is gonna come. I think its going to come down to bare bone survival I'm here to tell you with a minimum wage in place we have absolutely no chance of surviving.

There will be millions upon million starving to death and it could take civilization back to the Stone Age. The minimum wage and government regulations are blocking anyone from bartering and surviving on their own.

No one will escape and no amount of wealth is going to get you food if no one is willing to sell. Even if you have prepared and have food it would take an army to protect you with millions starving around you.

It is simple if there was no minimum wage at least the people could barter and do for each other just to eat if nothing more. But, with a minimum wage and countless big government regulations blocking you at every turn no amount of self-initiative is gonna keep you from starving.

As it is now the welfare state as a super family provider has nearly destroyed what has guaranteed human survival for over 5,000 years, the nuclear and extended family and its "Role" system.

Sure, opportunity and freedom to all is a must and no one doubts that in this great nation. But, who is going to raise the children and care for the sick and elderly when soon our big government will be totally broke with no borrowing power.

I'm telling you its not gong to get better like the egg heads and the elites keep promising, mass starvation is on its way whether we like it or not. I'm telling you we are about to face the sheer survival of the USA and western civilization itself.

I feel it is my destiny at all cost to get out the stress call for this nations survival no matter my handicaps and flaws. Agree or not I feel it is a calling and duty. I fear and hate the limelight. I also feel the minimum wage is standing in the way of this nation's survival.

All praise be to God. We shall survive. Minimum wage "I banish you" in the name of God.
SIRMANS LOG: 15 DECEMBER 2011, 0123 HOURS

SLAVERY IN ECONOMIC TERMS!
Slavery is still around in some isolated cases.
When you go back in history before western
civilization and private land ownership slavery
played a major role in economics.

I keep telling people a free market place with
free competition is the only way a nation can
feed its entire people. In economic terms
what freedom and the free market place
actually do is release two of the most
energizing forces in our human makeup.

Even today very few American understand
these two forces especially liberals because
on the surface they seem to go against the
grain of the status quo. If you lack wisdom
and perspective you won't understand these
two forces which is the case with the vast
majority of Americans.

The two forces I'm talking about are greed
and self-interest. Like electricity these two
forces are dangerous and can be deadly. The
key is to harness these two powerful forces
but never shut them down or hinder them too
much. Only a free market place will harness
this super powerful energy in a way that will
produce almost unlimited abundance in
everything.

Anybody following Keynesian Theory doesn't
know what the hell is going on in this day and
time in my view. I can dissect an economy

myself, and there is no doubt in my mind the welfare state cannot and will not survive, period.

Except for a free market place economy every other economic system tends to hinder or shutoff greed and self-interest. I predict within five years the world is going to experience slavery and starving in a major way. There is nothing complicated about it, it is simply human nature at work.

No one is going to be caring and do extra work when some one else is doing less and receiving an equal reward. Sure, using fear and pain will get some production but never abundance. In this nuclear weapon age no powerful nation can get away with taking over smaller weaker nations and working them like slaves like in the distance past.

So, without a true free market place economy I will guarantee you slavery will be back with a vengeance. With no one being able to make a profit due to big government there simply will be no other way for a nation to survive. I tell it as I see it. Praise be to God, Hallelujah. SIRMANS LOG: 11 DECEMBER 2011, 12 MIDNIGHT.
PS: The biggest problem with the USA is we have gotten too far away from a true free market place economy. It is impossible to have a true free market place economy with a minimum wage in place.

UNITED STATES POST OFFICE DEBACLE?
I have my own take on the U.S. Postal Service debacle and decided to weigh in on this matter. I can only give my one man opinion on what I think is going on. It may be sort of like social security with government siphoning off money for other government spending.

My belief is some of the money that should be going to the Postal service is probably being secretly siphoned off for other government spending. Unlike most government agencies the United States Postal service is a fee for service agency.

That being the case by all means the Postal service should be able to stand on its own. I think there is a lot more going on with the Postal Service than meets the eye. The first thing is I believe there are too many cooks in the management kitchen.

The second thing is I believe politics has a strangle hold on management with no one with any real power in charge of running the place. Sure, the unions are a factor and play a major role, still, with long term low interest loans there is no logical reason why the Postal Service can't survive without all of these cutbacks.

Come on! Give me a break! Like I said, I believe somewhere money is being siphoned off and spent elsewhere in the government; however, there is no way for me to prove that.
SIRMANS LOG: 7 DECEMBER 2011, 2148 HOURS

BOLD AND IN YOUR FACE!
In my view "The Bloom is off the rose, the cat is out of the bag," the progressive liberals are throwing rocks as always but now no longer feel a need to hide their hand anymore.

We can now see from top to bottom that the progressive liberals are openly promoting the "All for one and one for all" socialist and centralized communist like thinking. To them Individual freedom, small government, and a free market place all are seen as "The enemy of the people."

Plus, with a shallow economically ignorant predominate liberal news media riding shotgun they no longer feel a need to hide their real intent anymore. And with eighty years of false you-owe-me liberal entitlement mentality indoctrination they just may be right.

God I ask in your name, save the great USA.
SIRMANS LOG: 7 DECEMBER 2011, 0951 HOURS

PS: And another thing, I think giving the military the power to arrest civilians is a first step toward taking our guns away.

Sure, the liberals played the biggest role in birthing our welfare state. But, this nation didn't get on the brink of a total economic collapse with just liberals; a lot of conservatives took the course of least resistance and looked the other way.

We know as a rule liberals are basically shallow and live in the moment, but what can be just as dangerous to freedom is a shallow conservative, especially if he wants to give arresting power to the military to arrest civilians.

JUST A LITTLE INJECTION CONCERNING "PROFIT."

I have never considered myself to be an exceptional intelligent person, still, for the life of me I can't understand why I can dissect an economy so clearly while ninety five percent of the USA population just don't get it.

To understand economics all you need to do is understand one thing and that will be ninety five percent of the battle. That one thing is profit, profit, profit, and more profit. If you don't understand what profit is you are lost and don't know what wealth is either.

I will give a quick walk through background. In the beginning before the proper tools and weapons man spent most of his awake time hunting and searching for food. There was no profit because profit is the ability to have more than you need to live on.

Once farming reach the stage to store grain and domesticate animals then profit could be realized as long as one had enough for himself and family to get through the winter. Plus, seed stock and seed grain had to be maintained, and then whatever one had over that was called profit. So, in the final analysis it will always boil down to eating or starving.

You can't eat money or any material possession. All this big government and welfare state stuff ain't gonna feed anybody if not enough people are producing food. Why go into business when all your profit goes to someone else, it's not quite there yet, but it is getting harder and harder for any business to make a profit.

That's the problem with liberals, they don't give a damn what they destroy as long as they stay in power. But, in the end there will be no power to be had because there will not be anyone making any profit for government to take and survive on
Get a grip America! One hundred years ago the only place you could find a liberal was in a rich family or maybe on a college campus.

Now, the welfare state has made practical all of the poor hardcore liberals.

In over 5,000 years of written history when have the very poor ever been in favor of killing babies in the womb and men marring men, give me a break, people. And I'm supposed to be the nut case, here. I, Freddie L. Sirmans Senior will not shut up and look the other way.
SIRMANS LOG: 2 DECEMBER 2011, 2355 HOURS

IT'S TIME FOR SOME FORM OF LEGAL PROSTITUTION TO GET CONTROL OVER PORN IF NOTHING ELSE! I HAD GRAVE RESERVATIONS ABOUT ADDING THIS ARTICLE BUT DECIDED TO DO IT ANYWAY COMES WHAT MAY. THIS IS MY ONE MANS OPINIONS ON WHY I THINK PORN IS TOTALLY OUT OF CONTROL. VERY FEW AGREE WITH ME, BUT I STAND BY MY REASONING ON THIS.

LOOK AT WHAT IS HAPPENING TO SOME OF THE SOCIAL WEBSITES AND THE PERVERTED SEXUAL SMUT THAT MANY YOUNG KIDS HAVE TO WITNESS. I'M POWERLESS TO STOP ANYTHING BUT I WANT EVERYONE TO KNOW THAT I'M MORALLY AGAINST ALL THIS MORAL ROT AND DECAY.

JUST LIKE EVERYTHING ELSE MONEY AND

PAYING CUSTOMERS IS WHAT DRIVES THE PORN INDUSTRY. CLICK ON MY ARTICLE > http://flsirmans.blogspot.com/2007/08/is-illegal-prostitution-shutting-off.html SIRMANS LOG: 16 NOVEMBER 2011, 2357 HOURS

OHIO VOTE EQUALS MOB RULE ECONOMICALLY WISE!
"We have a republic if we can keep it." The founding fathers almost to a man believed that pure democracy was nothing more than mob rule, that is why we actually have a republic form of government.

The general public as a whole is almost always ignorant and uninformed on how to run a working government. It takes strong leadership that will proper educate the public and bring them along to have and keep a successful government in a free society.

Overall, I don't blame the citizens for what happened in Ohio. But, I do blame the progressive liberals that used the depression to seize the family provider role for itself and birthed the welfare state we have today. And as long as our government is in the provider role nothing or no one is going to stop it from taking the last red cent from anyone that makes a profit.

Riding shotgun for the progressive liberals is

the vast predominate liberal news media which has educated to some degree 95 percent of the general public with this false welfare state you-owe-me entitlement mentality.

I'm here to tell you, you can't get blood out of a turnip meaning because of too high taxes soon no one will be able to make a profit, then guess what, there will be no one making any profit for government to take in the form of taxes. Then a broke government ain't gonna be taking care of anyone. The people are supposed to be taking care of the government not the government taking care of the people in the first place.

The nuclear and extended family system have never failed to guarantee human survival in well over 5,000 years. But, here we are with our dumb asses putting all of our faith in a welfare state beast that dies with a broke government. And there has never been and never will be a government that doesn't go broke at some point. Also, according to the supreme law of nature when you take away the survival need for anything you make it extinct in time.

With the welfare state that is what we are doing to the nuclear and extended family system by slowly making it extinct. There must be a divine reason why a neurotic handicap like me came out of the woodworks to bring back some sanity before all of this shallow dumb insane thinking takes this great nation over a cliff.

Sure, the Ohio voters won their public employees union battle, but that will demand higher taxes. The unions may have won that battle but the whole state will loose the war when people begin starving.

Sure, the Ohio voters won their public employees union battle, but that will demand higher taxes. The unions may have won that battle but the whole state will loose the war when people begin starving.

When you kill the goose that lays the golden egg of profit with the scatter gun of higher and higher taxes, mass starvation always follow. Nature's supreme law of "Natural selection" guarantees that. And the reason we have never ending higher and higher taxes is because government is a family provider.

Sure, veteran and a few other pensioners is a good thing, but government should never become a mass family provider if it is to survive long term, because like any broke and desperate family provider it's going to lie, beg, borrow, or steal to feed its dependents. So, if you think our soon to be broke provider welfare state won't do something terrible and unimaginable you are fooling yourself.

However, government does have a duty as a last resort to make sure the poor and needy doesn't freeze or starve. But, the only way the government can help the poor and needy without destroying the free market place economy is to establish government run commissaries, housing, and clinics. And token or script must be used to prevent contamination of the nations currency.

Government should never under any condition give out free money or food stamps on an individual basis. The key is "Individual basis," because that act alone is what ignites consumer inflation by creating a bigger enough pool to allow high priced merchants to never have to lower their prices in order to stay in business.

That causes everyone to pay higher and higher prices and taxes in a never ending upward spiral, and it also destroys the buying power of the dollar in the process. No matter what the learned egg heads and elites may tell you, "I" say nothing else can ignite and driver consumer inflation out of sight like what is happening now, I double dog dare you, prove me wrong.

See my emergency USA survival blueprint > http://www.flsirmans.com/FLSirmansEmerge ncyUSAsurvivalBluePrint
SIRMANS LOG: 9 NOVEMBER 2011, 1815

HOURS

THE PHENOMENON OF "HERMAN CAIN" AS SEEN BY SELF-MADE WRITER FREDDIE L. SIRMANS, SR.

They say that life is a cycle and history repeats itself. And in this case we may again have two great African American men squaring off to shape the course of history, but in this case it is not about their race but the direction of the whole nation.

In the first case it was William E. B. Du Bois versus Booker T. Washington on which course the African American race would take. Washington believed that African Americans should take the self reliance route and focus first on learning the basic trade vocations to feed and control their own destiny.

He didn't put a priority on integration. On the other hand, Du bois disagreed openly in public with Washington and believed that African Americans should not be limited in anyway. Du bois believed that blacks should go the full integration route and focus on the best education possibly.

Du bois way won out on the course blacks should take. Sure, overall Du Bois way did win out in theory but it have never paned out in practice even to this day in my view.

However, this time around so much about America has greatly changed; African Americans are no longer the largest minority group anymore. Plus, in my view the ideology factor is even more the deciding factor than the race factor except for the fewer and fewer secret raciest.

In my view and backed by what I seen on a call in TV show, most of the most vicious attacks on Cain came from African American callers, even one black lady called him a monkey. Coming out of slavery and even to this day I don't think most African Americans have unconditional accepted a black identity.

I think still far too many African Americans see other blacks as competitors and in some cases the enemy instead of an honorable fellow independent authority figure. Why else would so many of us use the hated "N" word in private if not in public as if it doesn't apply to each of us personally.

I think the welfare state has locked most African Americans into a do-for-me dependent mode. I think one political party practical own the African American race, and that could never happen to a people that individually think for themselves.

That said, enough of me putting down my proud African American race. No one, no race, and no nation are perfect. When all is said and done, overall I truly believe the African American race to be one of the greatest people to ever exist. Sure, I may criticize and come down hard, but to me it is constructive criticism and done out of genuine love.

Against overwhelming odds and stripped of their culture, language, and religion these people withstood slavery and came out illiterate in a hostile environment with almost nothing. They didn't have the option to escape and blend in because of their color.

Still, they created Jazz, and have made great achievements in every phase of American life, they are survivors. And today we see a man of color in the White house, and even greater is a country that has allowed this unlimited freedom to happen.

At heart I'm a conservative, but in practice I behave more as a pragmatist or realist. A black conservative to a liberal is like someone shelving a Christian cross in the face of vampire. They screech and see it as a threat to their very being, and that same reaction also applies to the hordes of dependents depending on the liberals to stay in power.

The mass liberal media will never accept a genuine African American conservative in my view. They just can't understand why a black person in their view can reject their helpful do-good intentions. You see, it is all about control to them, a liberal loves controlling more than anything else because that adds a purpose to their life.

A self-sufficient do-for-yourself conservative black threatens the whole welfare state reason for being, and to a liberal there is no greater sin. To them he must be destroyed at all cost.

Which way will the nation go? Will it zoom warp speed into a failed socialist European like system or take the small government free market place course as the founding fathers designed the country to be, your vote matters, the future is in our hands.

PS: 2 NOVEMBER 2011, 0106 HOURS: BRIEF INJECTION:
I may be wrong on this, but if anything can pry the 90 percent plus loose this may be it the way the vicious partisan liberal media are going after this decent high moral black man. SIRMANS LOG: 30 OCTOBER 2011, 1343 HOURS

SIRMANS LOG: 4 DECEMBER 2011, 1745 HOURS
Well, Herman Cain decided to throw in the towel, who can blame him. That means there won't be a showdown between two men of

color for the president of the United States.

I think Dick Nixon said it best when he said "You won't have Richard Nixon to kick around anymore." Well, in my view the bias predominate liberal news media won't have "Ole Herman" to kick around anymore."

When I promise you the USA economy is going to collapse it really is a no brainier because it is the same as saying everybody is going to die. I understand it but the egg heads and the elites have tunnel vision and don't understand the role nature plays in economics.

Mother natures supreme law of "Natural selection" controls economics and everything else that exist. According to the law of natural selection there must be a survival need for anything to continue to exist, otherwise nature starts getting rid of it.

There is no survival need for moral decay and inefficiency, so it gotta go and if it means taking down a nation, too bad. Everything erodes or decays in some way and that includes ideas. Look at the great USA; it is now weighted down with moral decay, big government waste and inefficiency.

But, big government is much too powerful and will never allow small correcting purges that would cause much hardship but save the national economy. That is why nature's law of natural selection has no choice but to take down the nation's economy and maybe the whole world economy.

However, nothing in the future is ever written in stone man through his actions always has the power to determine his destiny. Throughout history there has never been a nation that changed course knowing it was headed toward disaster.

The reason is power never willingly concedes an inch; those wielding power will always go down with the ship. Due to the Rosetta stone we know that a written history and civilization goes back well over 5,000 years. The Roman Empire lasted a thousand years.

Ever since the dawn of history governments and rulers have always come and go, but, there was three constants over time that always stood firm until the "New deal" birthed the welfare state. Now, the whole of western civilization is on the ropes and may not survive all due to the infestation of the welfare state.

The three constants I'm talking about are the three pillars that allow human civilization to exist in my view: (1) A strong nuclear and extended family system, (2) a strong moral and religious code, (3) and adequate emergency bartering capacity with many, many small farmer and home gardeners in case the economy collapses.

Since the "New deal" birthed our welfare state we now depend almost entirely on our super provider welfare state from cradle to grave. Neglecting and dismissing the things that has safeguarded civilization for over 5,000 years to me is pass dumb and stupid, it is sheer madness. God forgive us.
SIRMANS LOG: 24 OCTOBER 2011, 2247 HOURS.

MY ANALYSIS ON WALL STREET OCCUPIERS! I believe what you see being played out with the Wall Street occupiers is a microcosmic example of what is being learned on the nation's universities and college's campuses.

I think almost 95 percent of the American people to some extent have bought into the liberal welfare state entitlement mentality. They call it the safety net and feeding the welfare state beast must be done to protect that at all cost.

This nation has been around 235 years and has always had to struggle with financial ups and downs but it was always armed with a strong nuclear and extended family system along with a good moral and religious code in place.

Starting with the "New deal" that birthed our welfare state we no longer have these solid foundation building blocks to withstand an all out struggle to survive as a free nation any more. Sure, we can keep feeding our tax hungry welfare state beast a little longer to buy time, but unless my blue print survival plan is taken seriously I see very little hope. See my emergency USA survival blueprint > http://www. flsirmans.com/FLSirmansEmergencyUSAsurvi valBluePrint

I believe what you see with the Wall Street occupiers are people with very weak survival instincts that have bought the liberal claptrap welfare state entitlement mentality lock stock and barrel. They don't care or even realize that with very few exceptions the rich got their money the hard way, they worked for it and made great sacrifices.

They don't realize that job don't just drop out of heaven. They don't realize that jobs are created by people just like you and I that didn't sit around waiting on someone else to act. These people took great financial risk and in most cases fought against great odds to provide a job for themselves and many, many others.

These people are our job providers and should be praised. And anyone attacking them is either ignorant or stupid in my view. Even the definition of what a job is has been distorted. Everybody is all hung up on thinking that a job must come with health and pension benefits, nonsense, that is something that started with our welfare state.

Sure, to get that is great but to get any job to survive should be the first priority. Myself, I blame everything that is causing our downfall on our welfare state. Today even someone with self-initiative have a mountain to climb because of all kind of government licenses and permits.

It is getting to where it is almost impossible for some one to start small. Starting small is what made America great? The old saying "Living of the land doesn't apply anymore. I don't know where it is all going to end, but, I do know without a doubt that our welfare state cannot and will not survive. God save America.
SIRMANS LOG: 23 OCTOBER 2011, 0104 HOURS

PS: And here is another thing I decided to comment on. But, let me say this first, I seldom comment on any politician or any individual. Here goes my take on governor Perry, I don't care what anyone says I believe it is what he said about social security that have hurt his chances to be president.

I, and many, many others totally agree that what he said was factual true, but we are not trying to become president of the united states. I remember when he first entered the race and zoomed right to the top. I, like most Americans knew only that he was a very successful Texas governor.

I have heard the old folks mention first impressions many times, but even now I never get carried away on something like that, the same as judging a book by the cover, but I guess in some cases it really does
matter.

Right after he called social security a ponzi scheme I thought to myself, wow, does he know the old folks are the biggest and most powerful voting block in the country, and social security is like a God to them?
So, in my view that statement was like spotting your opponent twenty paces from git go.

Sure, the pundits will be all over the map with all kinds of reasons why he can't get a leg up, but I believe unless he can find a way to defuse that social security statement nothing is going to work. There is no running away from it he must go for an all out repent of his sin and ask for complete forgiveness for speaking ill will against social security.

He must promise to never attack or speak ill will of social security ever again. Nothing short of getting the old folks to forgive him of his past social security beliefs are going to allow him to become president of these United States in my view.

There is no shame in just saying I was just plain wrong about social security, the old folks are a caring and forgiving people. Besides, there was one powerful bible character that spent years putting down Christianity but ended up being one of its greatest protectors.

I, Freddie L. Sirmans, Sr. I am a self-made writer that write what I truly think and believe, I could be wrong on this but that is my analysis.

EVERYBODY IS ALREADY PAYING TOO MUCH TAX, AND DEMONIZING THE RICH IS STUPID IN MY VIEW!
I found myself smiling while listening to a liberal lion go on and on about the rich not paying their fair share of taxes and blaming everything on the republicans.

Whereas, I know beyond a shadow of a doubt that it is the liberals claptrap garbage mentality that have brought this great country almost to its knees with this welfare state beast Lording it over all of us. The reason why I couldn't help but smile is because sometimes humor is the best way to defuse and accept a sad situation.

As I sat listening to this super liberal lion spout on and on the standard liberal blame shifting garbage it made me feel so befuddled and sad knowing nearly half of the nation is flimflammed by this stuff. I'm afraid it may be too late now history and our destruction is on the liberals side unless a miracle take place, its going to take some hard decisions and
hardship to save this nation and I'm not for sure we have the stomach for it.

I am almost alone yelling and hollering to deaf ears, no one want to hear me, when I yell get rid of the minimum wage and never give anyone money or food stamps on an individual basis, they think my God give wisdom is stupid. Still, I will never loose hope and stop trying to help save this great nation.

Like I have said many times before when it becomes almost totally acceptable to attack the rich, freedom and democracy is on its last leg, and I condemn anyone that does it. When you see entertainers, sport figures, business executives and others making extreme amounts of money that is because of big government and our welfare state, don't blame these people more power to them.

In a free market place economy with unhindered competition no extremes can get out of hand, only government can get between the merchant and the consumer and ignite consumer inflation by subsiding higher and higher prices enabling enough people to pay them. There never has been and never will be a rich and prosperous country without a lot of rich people to make it happen.

Poor people with money are not the same as rich people, there is a world of difference in mentality, plus almost all rich people have a strong sense of altruism, which is not the case with most of the very, very poor.
It may not seem so, but if you scratch below the surface of most genuine failures in life you will find a very self centered individual.

Without exceptions trying to make everyone equal in life will always make everyone equally poor except a very few privileged leaders. Look at history, the first thing every dictator or any power grabber does is go after and attack the rich, because they know the rich is the lifeblood of every democracy.

In a democracy the loyalty of the rich is a must because if the rich can't keep and hold on to their money they have the means to leave. I believe turning people against the rich is one of the most destructive things you can do to a free and democratic country. The old saying "Ways and actions speak louder than words" should wake people up but it doesn't.

Myself, I have been out here for years beating the bushes trying to drive the political snakes out into the opening, but to little or no avail. I think the liberals really mean well but human beings and what motivates them is something they have never understood.

Liberals just don't care or understand that when you do for and make a human being a dependent you destroy that persons will to survive on his own. Balance is the real key to human survival, to little struggle to survive can be as bad as too much hardship to survive.

One reason why we may loose our freedom is our lack of instilling good judgment and character in our young. I believe good sound judgment and character can only be instilled with a certain amount of real or imposed hardship and struggle. I'm not in favor of any harsh extreme hazing, but the idea comes from imposing some form of hardship to help build character.

Sure, many will disagree with me on the necessity of hardship and struggle to build character; still I stand my ground on this.

Why do you think drug use is so out of control in this country, character may not be the main factor but it definitely plays a role?

The struggle to survive in all species have evolved over thousands of years and when struggle is taken away life tends to become less appreciated and leaves an unfulfilled void. To a large extent that is what has happen to this great country, far too many people today have weak survival instincts.

Far too many people couldn't recognize a moral threat if it slapped them upside the head. Far too many feel, who care if a man marries a man or a woman, marries a woman. Far too many feel it is only a fetus, which cares; the welfare state is going to take care of me in my old age.

What they don't know is nothing or no one escapes nature's supreme law of "Natural selection" but only so long. Nature's supreme law of natural selection purges out moral decay, inefficiency, and waste through births and rebirths.

The world is entering the early stage of a rebirth, and I'm here to tell you any nation without a strong nuclear and extended family system, a strong moral and religious code, and some bartering capacity with small farmers and home gardeners will have little or no chance of surviving.

SIRMANS LOG: 17 OCTOBER 2011, 2045 HOURS.

EMERGENCY USA SURVIVAL BLUE PRINT.
I stump my shoe hard on the wood floor and slam my hat down on the floor, too! And think, damn, damn, damn! Can't somebody understand simple logic! I'm no genus, what I keep telling people is just simple logic, whatever happened to people with even a little perspective! Have the welfare state destroyed even that!

Here it is again in a nut shell, I'm talking about the core problem, the root problem, the heart of the matter, the eye of the storm or whatever you call it. No amount of money or anything you do is going to save the USA and our freedom as long as we have a super family provider welfare state beast in control.

Nothing and I mean nothing as long as government is giving out money and food stamps on an individual basis is going to save our economy simply because that act alone kills the free market and drives inflation.
So, until the government is out of the family provider role 9-9-9 or any revenue raising or anything else is going to saving our great nation.

A provider welfare state is like a giant snowball rolling down hill, nothing is going to stop it. The more it takes in taxes the more it's going to need to feed its growing list of dependents, it feeds on itself, the more it grows the more it demands in never ending new taxes. Look what it has already done to the great USA, It has already almost totally destroyed the African American nuclear family and the rest of the country is not too far behind.

It has ripped our morals to threads where the word marriage now means anything one want it to. And our culture has come to mean me first, I want mine, I want it all, and on and on it goes. With a provider welfare state more money simply means giving it more power to grow.

Feeding our welfare state beast is the root cause of jobs going overseas and the other stupid things that is happening today. Behind it all in truth is the liberal's blind insane need to keep our provider welfare state beast as their Lord and Master. Whether we admit it or not we all are slaves to this beast. I rest my case, there is no reason to go on and on, if you don't get the point by now you never will.

Here is my blue print, Congress and the President must first, completely get rid of the minimum wage. Next, void all regulations on businesses, and then add them back as needed. Next, establish government run commissaries, housing, and clinics and use token or script to prevent contaminating the nations free market economy. And finally, government must stop giving out free money and food stamps to anyone on an individual basis because that is what causes consume inflation and destroys the free market.

Also, all government spending and burdens should be limited to defense, treasure, state, interior, and only what the people can't do for themselves and collect taxes accordingly. In closing I suggest this blue print be taken seriously as a guide only. I am only trailblazing a path, with that I have done my duty.

I have no father control, may God bless this great nation. I am under no illusions, I know this blue print will be totally ignored; one reason is because U.S. Senators are no longer appointed by their states and the people are no longer the sole family providers. In reality whoever is the family providers actually rules and controls the country, it's just that simple in a free republic like ours. Cry me a river.

Now, in truth the welfare state has almost all of the real power. The states and the people can piss and moan and bitch all day long, but that's about all in terms of making real changes. Instead of the United States senators being controlled by their state governor and congressmen they owe their

real loyalty to special interest. And the people owe their real loyalty to who pays them, which is our welfare state with fewer and fewer exceptions.
SIRMANS LOG: 5 OCTOBER 2011, 1632 HOURS

9 OCTOBER 2011, 0844 HOURS, THIS INJECTION:
According to the U.S. constitution the military and protecting the nation is the first duty and priority of congress and the president. But, here we are today with a congress avoiding its duty by assigning it to a committee of six with OUR NATION SAVING military's neck on the chopping block.

In my one man's opinion that is a crying shame. My advice to congress is to take my advice and vote to eliminate the minimum wage right now, not tomorrow. That will get the ball rolling on saving our economy and the nation, God bless and keep a free America.

The constitution was originally designed for senators to represent the interest of their state government no one else's. That was the reason they were appointed instead of elected in the first place.

STIMULUS, STIMULUS, DUMB, DUMB, I

THINK!
To me a stimulus package is like putting paper money down a rat hole. All it does is make a bad situation worse. When a nation is spending almost twice as much as it is taking in it is insane to think more spending is the answer, it is impossible to spend your way out of debt.

I truly understand how an economy works and to me the answer is very simple. The first truth is government spending is the problem and until that is recognized and admitted there is no saving the USA and global economy. What congress and the president need to do first right now is recognize that this nation's survival is at stake and act accordingly.

Instead of going on silly financial wild goose chases, void all regulations on businesses right now. Next, completely eliminate the minimum wage. Next, set up temporary emergency government run commissaries, government run housing in all these empty buildings, government run clinics, and use tokens or script for all who qualify for these government
services.

Next, stop all government spending except for military and essential government only functions. I know to most this line of thinking will be seen as insane, but, I assure you the stimulus path will lead to guaranteed doom for the USA, or we end up as a debt slave owned and controlled by foreigners.

My way to salvation is only a suggested path to take it doesn't have be word for word like I say but the path is a way out of no way, a word to the wise should be sufficient. God bless America.

PS: This path will set the USA economy free and guarantee without a shadow of doubt that entrepreneurs and the free market will save this great nation with freedom intact, nothing else can do that.

We must place all of our faith and trust in the proven ideology of the "Free market place at work.
SIRMANS LOG: 1 SEPTEMBER 2011, 0846 HOURS

IS HURRICANES THE WRATH OF AN ANGRY GOD?
The ancients certainly thought so and came up with human sacrifices and all kinds of appeasements. Believe it or not, however, excluding the sacrifices there are still some that fall prey to that type of thinking.

Myself, to that type of thinking I say poppycock, hogwash, bullcrap, or some other tits on a boar hog like metaphor. It is all nonsense, what goes around comes around and that includes the works of Mother Nature. It also includes the working of every economy, too.

Every economy has a boon and bust cycle and sooner or later the bust cycle is going to come back around no matter how much scheming and fine tuning the egg heads does. That is just a fact of life.

So, when we become dumb and stupid and let the welfare state replace and destroy our bread and butter nuclear and extended family system that leaves us up S... Creek without a paddle.

Today when most people first read my writing they think I must be some kind of extreme right wing kook or loon that is out of touch. What they don't realize is one hundred years or so ago 95 percent of Americans though as I do.

The validity of a strong nuclear and extended family system with good morals and values haven't changed in five thousand years; it is we who have changed for the worst as a people since the "New deal" birthed our welfare state.

When the wood chopper gave up on trying to splitting a mighty oak block before walking away he decided to knee down and takes a closer look. And sure enough he could barely see it but there was a tiny beginning split. He realized all of his long hard effort had not been totally wasted.

I feel the same as the great wood chopper, except after all these years of my writing effort I still can't see any reward, I wish I could just quit and walk away and never look back, but, I know I must carry on as long as any life left in me. I guess if I can enlighten just one person it will have been worth it.
SIRMANS LOG: 30 AUGUST 2011, 1135 HOURS.

OMG! JUST WHAT I NEED! THE IRS!
I placed all of my faith in Turbotax for the last few filing years. Now, here comes the IRS hot on my tail and closing in fast. Hopefully, I will live and survive to write another day.

I'm not complaining I'm a big boy now, I can take it; I just hope I escape with my hide and not be skinned alive. Seriously, if its determine that I owe I will pay, I may be too proud to beg but I'm not too proud to pay. I have active duty served my country and will always gladly do my citizens duty.

As a writer, maybe some humor can be found here; I have shared so much about my life,

why close my life book on this. God bless and keep this great nation always.
SIRMANS LOG: 23 AUGUST 2011, 1806 HOURS.

GOD BLESSES OUR FEDERAL RESERVE!
This idea of getting rid of the Federal Reserve is just plain dumb and stupid. That is like saying get rid of the government. You can't have an organized society without government.

There must be a government to protect and safeguard the whole society. However, what I am against is a welfare state type of government, which I believe is unconstitutional. Without government means anarchy with every man for himself.

The same thing applies to the economy; there must be some type of organized money system. Otherwise, you are left with only trade and bartering to survive. These people talking about getting rid of the Federal Reserve are just plain ignorant, it is the best organized money system known to man.

What type of currency to use is left up to congress and the president? Maybe it's time congress and the president considers getting back to a genuine physical currency with its value in the currency itself. But, to seriously consider getting rid of the Federal Reserve is shallow and short sighted.

What you are going to replace it with, a feudal system with Lords and castles, I think not. Right or wrong that is my one man's opinion.
SIRMANS LOG: 21 AUGUST 2011, 0730 HOURS

FOOD STAMP'S DESTRUCTIVE POWER!
I place food stamps as the third most destructive force behind the "New deal" and the minimum wage to a genuine free market place economy.

Number one is the "New deal" when it started giving free unearned money to the poor. Sure, the poor must be helped as a last resort and not allowed to starve. But, if the free market place is to survive the government must never give out free unearned money to anyone.

The only way the government can help the poor and disadvantage without destroying the free market place is by temporary establishing government run commissaries, housing, and clinics. And even that should be done only as a last resort after the extended family, the church, the community, and all else has failed.

Otherwise a survival need for the nuclear and

extended family will be replaced by government and in time the nuclear family will cease to exist. The reason why that will in time kill every economy is because there are only two players in an economy; they are a seller and a buyer or merchant and consumer.

The government is only a necessary parasite needed to protect the whole society. Government has the power and the big guns and many times takes over and run the whole show, but only a free market place economy can feed its entire population.

In a free country if government would just stay with collecting taxes, protecting the country, and doing only what the people can't do for themselves the economy would police itself and produce far more than the population could use.

Mother Nature's supreme law of "Natural selection" would maintain a natural balance between the buyers and sellers and purge out inefficiency, moral decay and other anti-survival forces. But, when government takes its tax money and gives out on individual basis free unearned money and food stamps to the poor that creates enough people with the money to keep higher and higher priced merchants in business.

Then the government raises the taxes on the

higher and higher priced merchants and the merchants pass their extra cost on to the public in a never ending inflationary spiral. After the "New deal" and the government started giving out free unearned money on an individual basis that ignited inflation but by then government had tasted the God like power of being a super provider.

Then the die was cast and I don't believe big government ever intend to give up one inch of its cradle to grave God like great white father provider role come hell or high waters. When it comes to money it is not the amount that truly matters it is the buying power that really counts.

Once inflation kicks in higher taxes on merchants only means higher prices passed on to the public. I didn't research when the minimum wage was started but at some point government decided the minimum was a good idea, I totally disagree.

All the minimum wage does is remove the safety valve from a free market place economy, it is then like a vehicle with no reverse or a hot water heater with no pop off valve. Folks, now don't get me all twisted I know the things I criticize was genuine intended to help the poor and to a lesser extent get politicians elected.

I know food stamps was meant to be a good

thing but just like free unearned cash it is deadly destructive to a free market place economy when given out on an individual basis.

With government not giving out free money to the poor It is impossible for most merchants to charge more than the poor can pay and stay in business because there is never enough rich to keep commerce flowing. When government is not involved in the free market place that will keep the cost of living down to where the people can pay their on food and doctor bills.

When government do help the poor and disadvantage by establishing government run commissaries, housing, and clinics it should always use tokens or scripts. That will make sure government spending is kept separate and not contaminate the nation's economy in any way.
SIRMANS LOG: 17 AUGUST 2011, 1245 HOURS.

LAST CALL TO ELIMINATE THE MINIMUM WAGE!
The egg heads, the ruling class, and the elites all think I'm some kind of nut case that few knows about and I should be ignored out of existence,
wrong.

When I keep harping on completely eliminating the minimum wage they think I'm a fool and don't know what I am talking about, wrong. Eliminating the minimum wage is the only thing that is going to save western civilization by starving the welfare state beast out of its all powerful super provider role.

That and that alone can set the free market place free to save western civilization. Nothing else can do it. That act alone will permit the nuclear and extended family system to rebound along with good moral and plenty of emergency life sustaining bartering capacity. Otherwise, if we fail to eliminate the minimum wage western civilization is done.

It will very soon have zero chance of surviving. The reason is Mother Nature herself is going to use its supreme law of "Natural selection" to reset western civilization back to zero, in other words the Stone Age.

The welfare state has destroyed 90 percent of the foundation that holds every society together. And without the elimination of the minimum wage the welfare state will complete the job with 100 percent destruction. I'm talking about a 100 percent destruction of the nuclear and extended family system.

As to good ethics and morals, right now we

have men marring men and women marring women and before long good ethics and morals will be something found only in the history books. And the old standby of having adequate emergency backup bartering capacity in case the economy fails, meaning many, many small farmers and home gardeners, they are now like so many, sucking on the welfare state provider tit.

Just in case anyone is thinking that if things get out of hand martial law will be used to demand order by force, could be in for a rude awakening. At this point western civilization without eliminating the minimum wage soon won't have any foundation left to support civilization or an organized society.

That being the case no amount of authority can prevent total chaos back to the Stone Age. Only the elimination of the minimum wage can save what little that is left of a foundation to survive on and reverse course before going over the cliff and taking western civilization with it.

Of course, I know I will be ignored more than ever but I believe my great supernatural wisdom is God given. Go ahead a laugh and dismiss me as a bigger nut than ever, but, one thing is for sure "We all dance to the tune of a distance drummer." Glory is to God.

The real secret is, life is all about maintaining

a balance, and I know most of my views are too one sided and to the extreme, but only drastic thinking and actions at this late stage can create a middle balance.

Once the minimum wage is eliminated the next step is the government must never give out free money to help anyone on an individual basis. To help the poor, needy or anyone the government must establish temporary commissaries, housing, and clinics and use tokens or script for those that qualify.

That will prevent government spending from igniting inflation and destroying the free marking place like what is killing today's economy.I assure you sooner or later some nation is going to see the light and grab my no minimum wage lifeline wisdom, not every one is going to play Russian roulette with their nations' survival.
SIRMANS LOG: 07 AUGUST 2011, 0011 HOURS

"OOPS! THERE IT IS!"
Like I've said before, the liberals will see you in hell before they will cut spending and stop the growth of government. For whatever reasons, those pushing for the collapse of the USA and global economies, it may be all down hill from here.

I knew it, I knew it, the conservatives and others would not be able to withstand the pressure, now I guarantee you taxes are going to be raised on the fewer and fewer businesses left standing. Lord knows I hope I'm wrong on this, but I'm afraid this may be the final nail in the coffin before the sunsets of the USA and global economies.

Like a broken record I'm still at it on pleading for the eliminating of the minimum wage. I yell to the world this welfare state beast is out of control and is just too powerful and mighty. But like David with his stone and sling shot I promise you, the elimination of the "Minimum wage will bring this beast to its knees and put the people back in control over their government.

Nothing else is going to break its death grip on the USA and global economies. The dam is about to burst, and once the dominos start falling no one knows where it's going to end, it may be back to the Stone Age, and only God knows, God save America, Amen.
SIRMANS LOG: 02 AUGUST 2011, 1455 HOURS

THE FORGOTTEN, ONLY GUARANTEED PENSION!
What this entitlement generation has forgotten or don't even know is for over 5000 years your only survival pension was your

children.

Until around eighty years ago when the "New deal" and this monster size welfare state came about the nuclear and extended family system allowed civilization to exist for over 5000 years. It is not a perfect system but no society have ever survived and existed without it in the history of man kind.

In the USA except for maybe a few veterans almost no one was on the government dole before the "New deal" came along. Sure, in the beginning social security was a good thing for the elderly and the severely disadvantaged, but now every body and his brother is on it.

Those that put all of their faith in government don't know history, there has never been a government that didn't go broke at some point. To let this big government welfare state kill the nuclear family system by taking away it survival need like what is happening is not only dumb and stupid it is sheer madness.

Never put all of your survival eggs in one basket, especially a tax hungry out of control welfare state beast. The biggest problem now is the welfare state has produced so many dependents so long that nearly 40 percent of the population has no clue as how to survive using self-initiative.

I wish somebody would please show me how in the hell you are going to pay your way out of debt by going deeper into debt, like the liberals are trying to do.
SIRMANS LOG: 30 JULY 2011, 2025 HOURS.

MASS ECONOMIC IGNORANCE!
About 95 percent of the American people's knowledge of how an economy truly works can be compared to a little kid that believes grits and eggs come only from the grocery store.

Even most economist has bought into this liberal garbage claptrap entitlement mentality that started with the "New deal." But, I'm here to tell you there are no free rides in life somebody always pays.

All wealth originates from some type of trade or business transaction by the private sector, period. No wealth originates from government it is always taken from somebody or somewhere. The first rule in economic is "You can't get blood out of a turnip."

You can't eat money and if there are not enough people producing food there is going to be starvation no matter who the liberals blame. When a nation prevents the private sector from making a profit it cuts its own throat that is biting the hand that feeds it.

Only a free market place nation can create wealth and feed its entire people, all other economic systems leads to mass starvation, that is the history, you can look it up. But, when have a liberal ever had common sense, very seldom in my view.
SIRMANS LOG: 29 JULY 2011, 0859 HOURS

WELFARE STATE DEATH GRIP MUST BE BROKEN!
As I set back and watch all of the ado going on about raising the debt ceiling I just take the whole thing with a grain of salt. In the grand scheme of things it really doesn't matter if they raise it or not because all that is doing is buying just a wee little more time.

Either way it is not going to stop the welfare state from killing off both the USA and global economies. As a supposition example, if miraculous all of the USA's debt and financial problems were solved today, we as a nation will still be doomed.

The reason is money and lack of jobs are direct and obvious, but the real things that hold every society together is not so obvious and have rotted away to the very core because of the welfare state. Number one, the base and foundation for all human survival are the nuclear and extended family system.

Nothing can exist and be strong without a survival need, and the welfare state has took away that need for the strong nuclear family and left this great nation with no means to survive when the going get rough, and believe me tough times is just over the horizon. And the other two critical survival means of good morals and adequate emergency backup bartering capacity are practical nonexistence.

I know no one want to hear it, but I repeat again and again that the only thing that is going to save the USA and western civilization is the complete elimination of the minimum wage as a start. Nothing else can break the death grip the welfare state have on this nation's economic throat; otherwise the welfare state is going to finish off the kill. SIRMANS LOG: 23 JULY 2011, 0005 HOURS

INFLATION'S BIGGEST MYTH AND MISCONCEPTION!
The biggest misconception about inflation is that the mass printing of money by government is the cause of inflation, wrong. Government can print all of the money it wants to and that alone will not ignite the cost of living consumer inflation.

So, OK, the government prints up all of this

worthless money? But, in order to ignite inflation it has to get that money to enough people on an individual basis to corrupt the natural balance between the merchant and the consumer. Handing out free unearned money on an individual basis that and that alone is the cause of the cost of living consumer inflation.

That is why I keep screaming so loud that government should never give out free unearned money on an individual basis. Sure, as a last resort when the nuclear and extended family, the church, the community, and social organizations all fail then government must come to the rescue.
And even then government should help the poor by establishing government run commissaries, housing, and clinics, and using scrip or tokens to prevent destroying the USA national economy which has happened.

Now, about 80 years after the "New deal" and mass false shallow liberal thinking it is just the opposite with close to 95 percent of the American people looking to government as the first resort for survival help, Lord, what a shame. But, oh, no, my great God given wisdom is totally ignored, I don't believe the egg heads will ever detour from the gimmick laden economical course of least resistance we are on today.
SIRMANS LOG: 16 APRIL 2011, 1631 HOURS.

I was born during the war years in a little Georgia town off Highway U.S. 129 not far from the North Florida border. It was in the winter of `42, three days before Christmas, Dec. 22, 1942, in Stockton, Georgia. I was the forth of seven surviving children in a group of fourteen. Unfortunately seven of those children died before I was born. My early years were spent playing and enjoying life.

I remember vividly a little lake right beside Highway U.S. 84 that we used to play in as young kids. None of us could swim. We used to call it the clay hole. At the time I guess I was about ten or eleven years old. We didn't have any swimming trunks so we would all swim naked. The water was sort of dark, but we all felt safe once we were in the lake. The challenge was to watch for cars passing on the road or anybody walking by.

The regular gang included my brothers Buie C. and Bernard "Rip", my cousin J.E. Burgess, neighboring kids Spencer Bines and sometimes Bo Bo Brown and I. My older brother Marvin Elder and a few other older neighboring boys, Joe Louis Glover, Ellis Williams, and Johnny Lee "Sweet Pee" Dorsey were much too mature for our group. I can't remember if my younger brother, Jimmy, four years younger than I, would ever come along.

We would take off all of our clothes, hide in the nearby bushes, and as soon as the coast was clear we would run and dive into the lake. The deepest spot was not over three and a half feet. And one of our biggest fears was that some grownup would come down to the lake and stay, because we would be ashamed to come out of the lake naked. I can't remember who the lady was, but I remember she walked down from New Prospect Baptist Church about a quarter of a mile down the road.

She walked right to the edge of the lake and started chewing us all out. I guess she had some kind of insight into our fears and shames, because she would not leave; she was determined to wait us out. We were all cornered and ashamed to come out of the lake. So after what seemed like an hour, it was getting late in the evening. Lady or no lady, we decided to make a run for the bushes where our clothes were hidden.

Everyone was embarrassed, but we knew we couldn't stay in the lake till dark. My father was a domineering, unyielding type of individual. One of my first experiences with his unyielding stance was my bed-wetting. I was a bed-wetter until I was approximately six or seven years old. My father's way of dealing with bed-wetters was an automatic whipping, with no exceptions.

That's just the way it was. No matter how hard I tried, I could not stop wetting the bed. I kept getting older and kept getting whippings, and the gladdest day in my life was when I quit wetting the bed. That meant I would not be getting whipped almost every morning over something I could not avoid. It left emotional scars that are still with me to this day. It saddled me with a pitiful look that I hated, and caused me to harbor a secret inferiority complex all through childhood.

It left me with a neurotic pitiful look that would at times take over my brain like an epileptic seizure especially if I was very tired or stood before a large crowd of strangers. I have come a very long ways in mentally overcoming this handicap mostly through the positive thinking technique.

However, you never erase anything from the all powerful mind, all anyone can do with a handicap is face it down and learn to forgive and accept it, then you will survive. My battles with self-shame has been a lone internal war but I have no regrets; it has made me a better human being with an almost super mind in some ways. I thank you God for my life, health, and strength.

I felt I could not let anyone get too close because something was wrong with me, and if people saw how pitiful I could look they would reject me, laugh at me, or feel sorry for me. Each reaction was unacceptable. I just wanted to be normal and accepted, no more or no less. I guess I was around nine or ten when my family moved about four miles to my grandmother's farm.

There again I felt the effects of a completely domineering and unyielding father. My father didn't give any warning like, "Don't do that again." As a young aggressive kid, I was expected to act good, but I was branded a bad boy and I guess I acted the part, because over a two year span, it seemed like I would get a whipping almost every day for something or other. Then all of a sudden it stopped.

I guess my spirit was broken. To me it didn't seem like I was doing anything differently. All I knew was I was glad I was not getting whipped almost every day. All of my young life was not miserable; in fact overall I was a very happy kid. Then and now I never held anything against my dad or took it personally. Sure, my dad may have been somewhat too strict, but we are all human and no one is perfect, I can earnestly say that overall I knew him to be a good and decent man.

I thank God he taught us seven kids how to survive with pride and dignity. Not a one of us has ever spent time in jail, and we are all over fifty. We all work to earn our keep, and we don't want or expect handouts from the government or anybody. It was mainly a matter of ignorance. My father raised me like his father raised him, and his father before him. Besides, the older I get the more I appreciate a strict rising, but not one without love.

If I had to choose between a rising of over-permissiveness or over strictness, I would choose the latter. It assures the best chance of survival under all conditions, but a balance between the two is always the most productive. I'd never be too hard on misfortunes, because they may save one from a more disastrous or fatal end. Just remember the Lord works in mysterious ways.

Sometime when one is rushing to get some place and nothing seems to work right, who knows that delay may have saved one from a fatal accident. Life is all about timing. Maybe not all, but some of us have a destiny, and must be prepared for the mission. I feel it is something bigger than an individual; even bigger than life itself. Like an idea whose time has come, it can't be held back, but so long, it has to happen.

In spite of my handicaps I have long known my mission and destiny must be something almost out of this world big, just maybe, it may be to help save western civilization in a recognizable way, little ole me. Praise is to God.

In 1955 they closed the two-classroom school house in Stockton, Ga., and I attended the seventh grade over in Lakeland, Ga., the county seat. We sharecropped the farm one more year with Isben Livingston that my grandmother's heirs had sold him the year before. Then in the summer of `56, the Charlie Sirmans' family moved from Stockton, Ga. to Valdosta, Ga... There my father became a taxi driver. Mother dear, Alberta, a lovely, non-complaining, passive woman was in frail health.

She had suffered the first of her many strokes. I attended the segregated Pinevale High School. I excelled in basketball and football. I was a member of the Pinevale Tigers basketball team. I can still cock my head and imagine hearing the basketball cheerleaders chanting, "Freddie! Freddie! Freddie! He's our man, if he can't do it nobody can." I finished high school in 1961 and turned down a basketball scholarship to attend Fort Valley State College in Georgia.

It was the alma mater of my late high school basketball and football coach, Edward Jones of Quitman, Ga. He believed in me and thought very highly of me. I will always remember how he walked to my house in the rain to bring me the news of my basketball scholarship. The only other member on the basketball team to get a scholarship that year was Oswell Jones, who went into the U.S. Army.

I later went into the U.S. Air Force. I worked a while at South Ga. Pecan factory in Valdosta, Ga., and then about the middle of 1962 I decided to move to Tallahassee, Florida, to attend a trade school. The name of the school was Consolidated Electronics. I went to the school about two hours a day, and got a job in a little delicatessen and donut shop on Adams Street near the old capitol building.

I rented a room from a lady named Mrs. Ford who lived right in front of the funeral home on Carolina St. I stayed there for about six months until the school ended.
After returning to Valdosta in late 1962, I decided to enlist in the U.S. Air Force.
Being a young man, I spent some of my leisure time cruising North 24th Street in Omaha, Nebraska. At that time there were two nightclubs we used to hang out in, the M&M Lounge and the Off Beat Lounge.

Then I moved on to Puerto Rico for my last two years in the military. While there, I bought an old 1952 Studebaker. I still have fond memories of the Caribbean and the tropical climate. Still young and enjoying life sometimes we would check out Isabella, but mostly we would hang out in the little coastal town named Aguadilla. At that time in Aguadilla they had a night club called the Black Stallion where most of the airmen hung-out.

I distinctly remember they had one famous patron called Casa Boo Boo (house ghost). She was as black as the ace of spades and very ugly, but she must have made up for it in other ways because she always got her share of dates. In 1966, after four years in the U.S. Air Force I got out and returned to Valdosta. I had turned down my basketball scholarship, so my goal was to get a college education.

At that time they had a four year, fully paid GI Bill that would pay you while you attended school. Then I missed my ship again. I got a job, got married and started a family. I don't regret anything. Now more than twenty five years later, and over age fifty, I feel maybe I have something worthwhile to say. I wrote a few letters to the editor that gave me some courage. Now here I am after writing four books and reprinting my first book.

I'm no intellectual; I am a high school graduate with one semester of college while in service. But I have done a fair amount of reading along the way. My writing should be raw, crude, and pure, so hang on for a ride.

YEAR 2011 ADD-ON:
First, let me take this time to count my blessings. Lord I have so much to be thankful for, I have a great family that loves me dearly. Thank you God, thank you, thank you for my life health and strength. This once beaten down pitiful little South Georgia USA country boy has kept the faith and is still standing. "May the life I have lived and the works I have done speak for me," thank you God, thank you.

On this day in the year of our Lord Twenty Eleven A.D. Saturday the first day of October, I, Freddie Lee Sirmans Senior again just took time to count my blessings. Three days before this Christmas I will celebrate my sixty ninth birthday December 22, 2011. However, still the effects of my childhood bed wetting punishment days at times haunt me. There are no doubt the mental scars and effects will go with me to my grave.

I, so much like everyone want to be proud and stand proud, but for me sometimes it is still a great struggle, the helplessness neurotic pitiful look still tugs at my soul. To me it is all about survival, I accept no excuses or blames for survival because I believe if you are looking you can always find an excuse for failure. I have fought mental battles to survive practical all of my life, and will never surrender. It is said that behind every super achiever there is a search for love and acceptance, I believe that.

"To try and keep trying is the greatest of all virtues. Winners don't quit and quitters don't win." Think you for taking the time to read about me, with love always, Freddie L. Sirmans, Sr.

****
****
Version #2 has additional information.
I was born in the early forties in a quiet little Georgia town near the Florida border.
It is located at the intersection of U.S. Highway 84 east to west and U.S. Highway 129 north to south. I was delivered by a midwife three days before Christmas, December 22, 1942 in Stockton, Georgia. I was somewhat puny and was not expected to live. I was the eleventh child in a group that would eventually reach fourteen children.

Unfortunately seven of those fourteen children died before I was born. I was a very sensitive kid, always snotty nosed, but I survived. The old frame house that we lived in was like many houses built around the turn of the century. The kitchen was separated from the living quarters of the main house. In our house, in order to get to the kitchen, you had to go outside and walk down a long porch to reach the kitchen.

We didn't have electric lights, and I remember at night someone older had to carry a kerosene lamp down that seemingly long, long porch, and I would be so afraid. One of my earliest memories in that old house was that I would get a whipping almost every morning for wetting the bed.

It left me with a neurotic pitiful look that would at times take over my brain like an epileptic seizure especially if I was very tired or stood before a large crowd of strangers. I have come a very long ways in mentally overcoming this handicap mostly through the positive thinking technique.

However, you never erase anything from the all powerful mind, all anyone can do with a handicap is face it down and learn to forgive and accept it, then you will survive. My battles with self-shame has been a lone internal war but I have no regrets; it has made me a better human being with an almost super mind in some ways. I thank you God for my life, health, and strength.

I remember we had a fireplace, and one morning I was standing with my back to it warming up. I had on some ragged bib overalls. All of a sudden I felt something hot on my leg, and when I looked down, I saw that my pant's leg was on fire.

I took off like a bat out of hell not thinking to smother the fire. I could have easily sustained third degree burns all over my body or lost my life because I would never have stopped running. Fortunately, there was a bed in the room and I ran into it, thereby allowing enough time for my sister Betty and brother Buie to reach me and smother the fire. A large burn mark still covers most of my left leg today. I hated short pants.

It seems as if I was fifteen years old before my mother would let me wear long pants. Most kids my age were wearing long pants, and I felt only little kids wore short pants. I wanted to be mature and grown up, not a little kid in short pants. Most of my earlier years were spent playing and going to the clay hole in the summer. The clay hole was a little man-made lake right beside U.S. Highway 84. Also about one quarter of a mile down the road was New Prospect Baptist Church.

It was at the church where I had to wear short pants and say an Easter speech every Easter. The regular members of the swimming gang were my brothers Buie and Bernard (Rip), my cousin J.E. Burgess, the neighbor kid Spencer Bines, sometimes BoBo Brown, and I. My older brother Marvin was much too mature for us. Our house was the old Corbin home. My grandfather Henry Corbin had moved to Waycross to work for the railroad years ago.

I guess I was around nine or ten when the family left the old Corbin home and moved about four miles to my grandmother's farm. It was the Sirmans' home place that my great-grandfather Steve "Buck", a slave, settled on when he became a free man. My grandmother, Alice Roberts Sirmans, who was born about 15 miles away in Mayday, Georgia, was half Cherokee Indian and half white.

She had been living at the farm when we moved in but moved shortly thereafter to a house in Valdosta, Georgia that my father Charlie and my uncle Freddie had recently built. There on the farm I was expected to do my share of the work. I remember very clearly that complaining did very little good. I remember we had to pick up sweet potatoes after they had been plowed from under the ground.

You had to stay bent over for long periods of time. I would tell my mom or dad that my back was hurting, and they would say, "Boy! What do you mean your back is hurting? You don't even have a back at your age. All you got is gristle." I cropped tobacco and hung it in the barn, but the most hated job was gathering corn in beggar weeds. The corn and the beggar weeds would cause your skin to sting.

Then around 1954 the Sirmans' heirs got together and sold 100 acres of our farm land to Isben Livingston. My dad bought the other 100 acres of the wood land that our house was on which he sold a few years later. In 1955 they closed the two classroom school house in Stockton, Georgia and I attended the seventh grade over in Lakeland, Georgia the county seat. Then in 1956 the Charlie Sirmans' family moved to Valdosta, Georgia.

My dad became a taxi driver. That year I was in the eighth grade, and I started the school year in the old Dasher High School that had been downgraded to a junior high school. At that time a strong disciplinarian, highly moral, and spiritual man, patrolled the halls. That man was Professor J.L. Lomax, the principal, whom the school was later named after. I, like the other students, was terrified and scared to death of being caught in the hall unauthorized.

The new school, Pinedale High, had just been completed. For some reason, I can't remember exactly why, they had added two eighth grade classes to the new high school that first year. Thereafter it was only grades ninth through twelfth. I was in one of the two eighth grade classes attending that first year in 1956. I believe my home room teacher was Ms. Carrie Lissimore.

The principal, Mr. C.C. Hall, the late band director, Mr. C.D Marshall, the chorus and others agreed that the school's new anthem did not rhyme properly with the word Pinedale. Everyone agreed that Pinevale rhymed almost perfectly with the new anthem, so the school was thereafter known as Pinevale High. "Good old Pinevale High we will live and die for you, for you."

I was very insecure and shy in high school and will probably be somewhat shy and insecure all my life. I remember very vividly an incident that happened to me in Ms. Sarah Jones' class. I guess I was in the eleventh or twelfth grade. I had my shoes leaned on their side under my desk, and when I shifted their position on the tile floor it sounded just like someone passing gas. All eyes focused on me, but I never looked up, I just kept my head hung and bowed.

After what seemed like a slow motion minute, Ms. Jones casually and quietly walked over and opened some windows near where I was sitting. After the class was over a small lad that sat right next to me, I can't remember his name, but he walked up and told me, "I know that was your shoe that made that noise" and I told him that it truly was. The reason I mention this incident is that because of my shyness and insecurity at the time I failed to set the record straight.

Even if I didn't have the courage to speak up then, I should have at least gone to Ms. Jones later and set the record straight. But instead I remained mute, and to this day as far as I know only that young lad in that whole class knows that I was innocent. Unlike most of today's young men, I was a late bloomer. I had come close, but when I finished high school I had not had a consummated relationship. In fact, my first consummated relationship came around the age of twenty.

In high school I was a jock. I was crazy about girls, but I was afraid to go after them. I excelled in sports, so that became my primary interest. When I graduated in 1961, only two members on the basketball team received scholarships, Oswell Jones and I. We each received basketball scholarships to Fort Valley State. We used to call Oswell the Big "O". To this day I can honestly say Oswell was one of the best basketball shooters I have ever seen.

Even in high school if he got hot he could consistently hit 25 foot jumpers. I am sad to say that he was a victim in a fatal car accident while returning to Atlanta from the "92" Valdosta High School Wildcats State AAAA Championship football game, which Valdosta won. I can still remember one of the chants that the Pinevale High basketball cheerleaders would yell out. "Freddie!

Freddie! Freddie! He's is our man, if he can't do it nobody can!"

I finished high school in 1961 and then worked a while at South Georgia Pecan Factory in Valdosta before moving on to Tallahassee, Florida to attend a little trade school. The name of the trade school was Consolidated Electronics. I went to the school about two hours a day. I managed to get a job in a little bakery and delicatessen shop on Adams Street right around the corner from the old capital building.

I got a room with Mrs. Ford who lived right in front of a funeral home in French Town on Carolina Street. I stayed in Tallahassee for six months until the little trade school ended. After I returned to Valdosta in late 1962, I decided to enlist in the U.S. Air Force. Like most new recruits in basic training, I visited the Alamo in San Antonio. From there I spent two years in Omaha, Nebraska. At that time, GI's didn't make as much money as they do today, but we knew how to party on what we had.

THE END

Crude Self-made Writer
Freddie L Sirmans Sr
Website: FLSirmans.com

www.ingramcontent.com/pod-product-compliance
Lightning Source LLC
Chambersburg PA
CBHW051335170526
45166CB00002B/829